SEP 2012

S0-BYT-337

CHECKERBOARD SCIENCE LIBRARY

EVERYDAY INVENTIONS

TELEPHONES

EVERYDAY INVENTIONS

Kristin Petrie
ABDO Publishing Company

EAST NORTHPORT PUBLIC LIBRARY
EAST NORTHPORT, NEW YORK

visit us at
www.abdopublishing.com

Published by ABDO Publishing Company, 8000 West 78th Street, Edina, Minnesota 55439.
Copyright © 2009 by Abdo Consulting Group, Inc. International copyrights reserved in all
countries. No part of this book may be reproduced in any form without written permission from the
publisher. The Checkerboard Library™ is a trademark and logo of ABDO Publishing Company.

Printed in the United States.

Cover Photo: Alamy
Interior Photos: Alamy pp. 8, 10, 17, 23, 27, 28; AP Images pp. 9, 25; Corbis p. 12; Getty Images
    pp. 5, 11, 13, 29, 31; iStockphoto pp. 1, 14, 15, 22; Peter Arnold p. 16; Photo Researchers
    pp. 18–19

Image on page 21 reprinted with permission from *Britannica Elementary Encyclopedia*, © 2006 by
    Encyclopædia Britannica, Inc.

Series Coordinator: Megan M. Gunderson
Editors: Rochelle Baltzer, Megan M. Gunderson
Art Direction & Cover Design: Neil Klinepier

Library of Congress Cataloging-in-Publication Data

Petrie, Kristin, 1970-
  Telephones / Kristin Petrie.
      p. cm. -- (Everyday inventions)
  Includes bibliographical references and index.
  ISBN 978-1-60453-088-9
  1. Telephone--Juvenile literature. I. Title.

  TK6165.P48 2009
  621.386--dc22

                                2008001561

CONTENTS

Telephones 4

Timeline 6

Telephone Facts 7

First Steps 8

Voices from Afar 10

Bits and Pieces 14

Traveling Sound 20

Old and New 24

Staying Connected 26

Safe Communication 28

Glossary 30

Web Sites 31

Index 32

Telephones

Have you spoken on the telephone today? If you have, you probably didn't give this action a second thought. Today, the convenience of telephones is second nature to most people.

Thanks to the telephone, you can catch up with friends any time. All you need to do is pick up the telephone and dial! In fact, being in touch is a major part of everyday life. There is rarely a time when communication is not possible.

Do you rely on telephones? If you're not sure, try going several hours without using one. Note how often you would like to make a call. Soon, you will notice the importance of the telephone in your life.

Now you have an idea of how much you use the telephone. Next, think a little deeper. Who do you usually call? If you look around, can you see them from where you stand? Probably not.

This is why the telephone really comes in handy. Keep reading to find out where this invention comes from and how it works today!

Now that telephones are portable, you can talk to people from wherever you go. How often do you see someone talking on a telephone?

Timeline

1876	On March 7, Alexander Graham Bell received a patent for his telephone; on March 10, he placed the first telephone call.
1877	Bell Telephone Company was founded; Emile Berliner invented an improved transmitter for the telephone; Thomas A. Edison also invented an improved transmitter.
1891	London, England, and Paris, France, became the first international cities connected by telephone.
1896	Rotary dial telephones were invented.
1956	Undersea telephone cables linked North America and Europe.
1963	Touch-tone dialing began.
1964	Undersea telephone cables linked North America to Japan through Hawaii.
1979	Japan launched the first cellular telephone service.
1983	The United States launched cellular telephone service.

Telephone Facts

◯ In 1879, Rutherford B. Hayes became the first U.S. president to have a telephone installed in the White House.

◯ An inventor named Elisha Gray also claimed to have invented the telephone. In 1876, Gray notified the patent office that he was working on a speech-transmitting device. However, Alexander Graham Bell's telephone patent had been filed just a few hours before!

◯ Traditional telephones will still work during a power outage. This is because wires connect them directly to the telephone company. Through those wires, the telephone company provides enough power to run your telephone.

◯ Some cellular telephone towers are shaped like cacti or trees. That way, they blend in with the landscape!

First Steps

The word *telephone* comes from two Greek words. *Tele* means "far." *Phone* means "sound." Before this wonderful invention, there were no voices from afar.

Sure, people could wave flags or use smoke **signals**. They could also send letters in the mail. But what if they wanted to hear people speaking? They had to be right in front of them. Thankfully, early inventors were interested in more than just speaking in person.

The development of electricity in the 1800s made long-distance communication possible. The **telegraph** was an important early mode of electric, long-distance communication. **Morse code** messages

Samuel F.B. Morse developed the telegraph and Morse code in the 1830s.

became electrical **signals** that were sent along wires. By the 1840s, electric communication over the miles was a reality!

Unfortunately, **telegraph** technology was limited. At first, only one message could be sent at a time. Also, **Morse code** messages still took longer than spoken messages. The search for easier, faster two-way communication was on. That is when a young teacher from Scotland stepped into the picture.

Semaphore is a type of signaling that uses flags. It is still practiced today by organizations such as the U.S. Navy.

Voices from Afar

Alexander Graham Bell was a Scottish educator, scientist, and inventor. He studied communication and languages in his homeland and in England. In the 1870s, Bell **immigrated** to Canada. Then, he moved to the United States.

Bell had a great interest in both communication and electricity. He put these interests together to create the first telephone. Bell received a **patent** for his invention on March 7, 1876.

On March 10, Thomas A. Watson received the first telephone call. Watson was

Alexander Graham Bell was just 29 years old when he received his patent for the telephone.

Thomas A. Watson

Bell's assistant and coinventor of the telephone.

As they prepared to test the device that day, Bell spilled battery acid. He said, "Mr. Watson, come here. I want you!" As Bell spoke, Watson heard these famous first words clearly through the telephone!

Bell's invention was a great success. In fact, he founded the first telephone company on July 9, 1877. Inventors and scholars flocked to see the telephone. Yet, many inventors thought Bell's telephone should have a better transmitter.

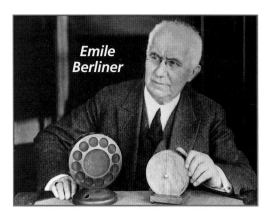

Emile Berliner

American inventor Emile Berliner invented an improved transmitter in 1877. It was one of the world's first **microphones**. Bell Telephone Company quickly bought the **patent** to Berliner's transmitter.

Thomas A. Edison was another great American inventor. He is best known for his work with the electric lightbulb. However, one of his early successes was improving Bell's telephone. In 1877, he also invented an improved transmitter. It made a person's voice louder and clearer.

Soon, international telephone calls became possible. In 1891, telephone service connected London, England, and Paris, France. This was the first telephone service between two countries.

Thomas Edison received more than 1,000 U.S. patents for his inventions.

Next, undersea telephone cables connected continents. By 1956, North America was linked to Europe. And in 1964, North America was connected to Japan by way of Hawaii.

Then in 1979, Japan launched the first cellular telephone service. The United States followed in 1983. Today, cellular telephones have become more popular than ever!

Bits and Pieces

On a rotary telephone, the numbers are set in a circle.

In order to function, telephones need a source of power. Older telephones get power from the telephone line. This is connected to the telephone base by a cord.

Newer, cordless telephones are battery powered. The battery charges when the telephone is on the base unit. This unit is usually plugged into an electrical outlet. Cellular telephones also operate with rechargeable batteries.

A switch hook controls the flow of electricity to a telephone. When you pick up a telephone handset, the switch hook lets electricity flow in. When you hang up, the switch hook turns it off.

Returning the handset to the base interrupts the flow of electricity. Lifting a telephone off its base is like turning it on. A dial tone is the **signal** that the connection has been restored.

The dialer is the set of numbers used to dial a telephone number. On rotary telephones, the dialer is a disk on a spring. The dialer creates pulses for each number as it turns.

Newer telephones have a keypad in place of a rotary dialer. A keypad creates **unique** tones for each number pressed. These tones tell the telephone company who you wish to call.

Before making a call, first listen for the dial tone. Then, dial a telephone number. This sends the telephone company a code made up of pairs of tones.

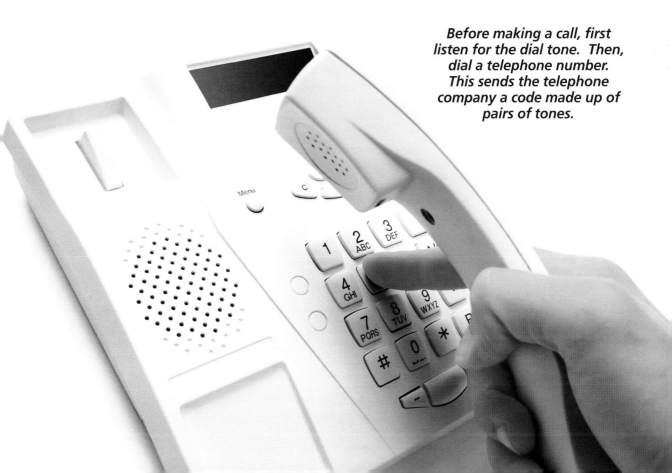

The telephone's ringer announces an incoming call. Today, your telephone's ringer can sound like just about anything! It can be a traditional bell, your favorite song, or a vibration.

A telephone transmitter is also called a **microphone**. Its job is to change the sound entering the telephone into electrical **signals**. That way, the sound can travel on telephone wires.

In a telephone handset, the microphone is the part you talk into. The speaker is the part you hold up to your ear.

A telephone's receiver, or speaker, receives the electrical **signals**. It does the opposite job of the transmitter. The receiver changes the electrical signals back into sounds you can understand. At the heart of all these parts is the printed circuit board. This is where many of a telephone's electronic parts are connected. A circuit board controls the flow of electricity through a device. In a telephone, it **coordinates** the functions of the parts named above.

A cellular telephone's circuit board has a microprocessor. Just like in a computer, this is the telephone's brain. It controls everything, including playing the right sounds to let you know you have a call!

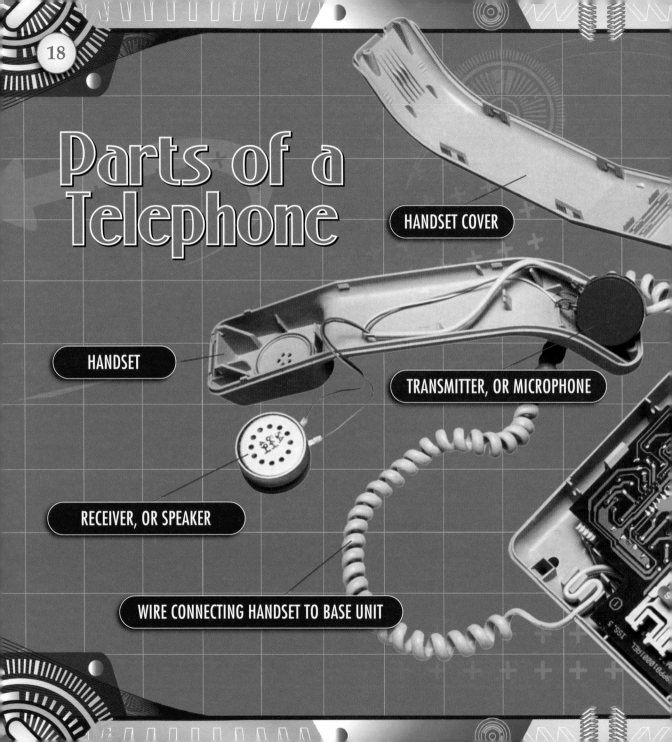

Parts of a Telephone

HANDSET COVER

HANDSET

TRANSMITTER, OR MICROPHONE

RECEIVER, OR SPEAKER

WIRE CONNECTING HANDSET TO BASE UNIT

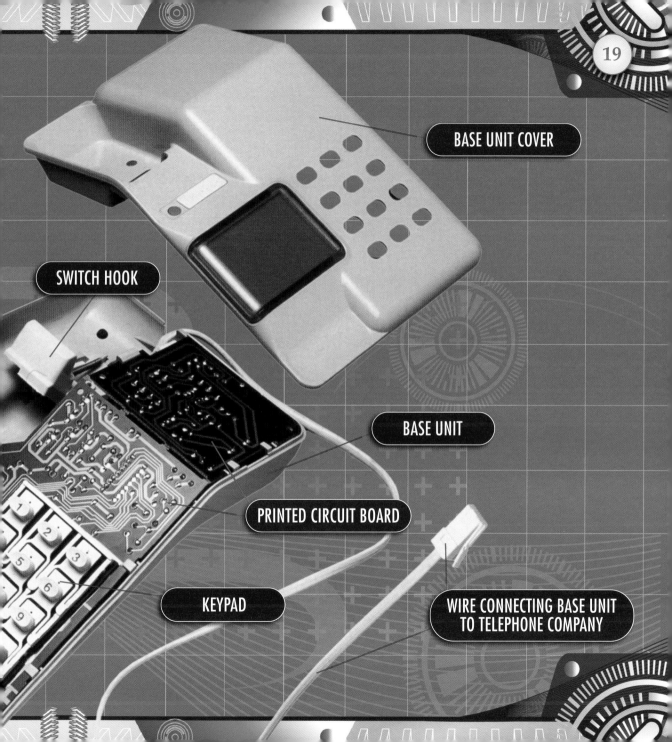

BASE UNIT COVER

SWITCH HOOK

BASE UNIT

PRINTED CIRCUIT BOARD

KEYPAD

WIRE CONNECTING BASE UNIT TO TELEPHONE COMPANY

Traveling Sound

What happens when you pick up a telephone to answer a call? First, the sound of your voice must be changed into something that can travel on wires. For this reason, sound is changed into electrical **signals**.

This change begins at the telephone's **microphone**. Inside the microphone is a **diaphragm**. This is a thin piece of metal. In older telephones, a cavity contains bits of carbon on the other side of the diaphragm. Newer telephones simply have two thin sheets of metal. One sheet acts as the diaphragm.

Each time sound enters the microphone, it causes the diaphragm to vibrate. In older telephones, this causes the carbon pieces to move. In modern telephones, the electrical field between the two metal plates changes.

These vibrations create changes in the electric **current**. The changes are a copy of the sound that entered the telephone. Meanwhile, an anti-sidetone circuit is hard at work. It makes sure you don't hear your own voice coming back out of the receiver.

How a Phone Sends and Receives Sound

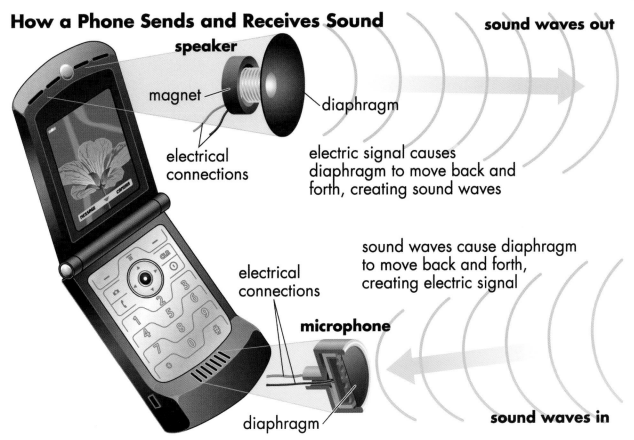

speaker

magnet

diaphragm

electrical connections

electric signal causes diaphragm to move back and forth, creating sound waves

sound waves out

sound waves cause diaphragm to move back and forth, creating electric signal

electrical connections

microphone

diaphragm

sound waves in

Next, the electric **current** travels to wires. These lead to a telephone network, a telephone company, and switching centers. They direct the **signal** to the telephone you are calling.

When the correct receiver is found, the electrical **signal** enters the telephone. Inside the telephone, the **current** affects a magnet wound with wire coils. This causes the speaker's **diaphragm** to vibrate. These vibrations return the current to the original sounds, your voice!

Telephone technology has changed a lot since telephones were invented. Newer telephones no longer use carbon pieces. A variety of ringtones have replaced the old mechanical bell ringer. Also, keypad dialing has replaced rotary dialing.

Newer telephones usually have a display screen. It can show numbers or even images. This allows for features such as caller identification, or caller ID. Your telephone screen displays the name and number of the person calling. Advances such as these make modern telephones small, **portable**, and fun!

Telephone signals are both sent and received through the wires that connect your telephone to the network.

A cellular telephone's display screen can show text messages. Rather than spoken words, these are written messages transmitted by telephone.

COOL C U TOMOZ AFTER SKOOL LUV YA!

Options

Clear

Old and New

Some of the first telephones used rotary dials. These were invented in 1896. Rotary dials have holes that each correspond to a number. Each turn of the dial sends electrical pulses to a telephone network.

The most common telephone today is the touch-tone telephone. Touch-tone dialing began in 1963. To use these telephones, callers press numbered buttons on the telephone's keypad. Each numbered button corresponds to a **unique** pair of tones. The telephone network uses the pattern of tones to route your call.

Telephones use cables to transmit telephone **signals**. Today, fiber-optic cables are quickly replacing old copper wiring. Fiber-optic cables are made of ultrathin glass. They can carry millions of signals at one time.

Cordless telephones are handheld telephones that use an antenna. They do not send information through a cord. Instead, the antenna transmits radio signals through the air.

These **signals** then enter a nearby telephone base unit. This allows callers to move freely within the antenna's range.

Cellular telephones use radio waves to transmit calls. This technology allows callers to communicate without the **restriction** of telephone lines. Instead, they rely on a nearby radio tower to route calls.

Cellular telephones get their name from the area each radio tower covers. These areas are called cells.

Staying Connected

Telephone professionals have a variety of jobs. A telephone operator helps you with your telephone call. Today, you rarely hear an operator's voice. This is because most services are run by computers.

However, operators are still available if the computer can't understand your needs. For example, an operator may help you make an international call.

What do you do when your telephone doesn't work? Use someone else's telephone to call a telephone repairer! Is there a problem with your telephone? Or, is the problem with the telephone line? Today's advanced technology makes these problems challenging. But, repairers are well trained so they can solve any problem.

What if a business needs an entirely new telephone system? This is where **telecommunications** salespeople and installers get to work. There are many options to consider when choosing a telephone system. Salespeople guide buyers through these numerous decisions. Then, an installer sets everything up.

Sometimes, climbing a telephone pole is necessary to connect a new line or repair a broken one. But, leave this to the professionals!

Safe Communication

Did you attempt to go without a telephone for several hours? If you did, this invention's importance in your life is probably clear. Telephones help you keep in touch. They put information at your fingertips and at your ears!

In the world around you, telephone technology is vital. Governments remain in constant communication to

Telephones aren't just for calling anymore! Today, you can use telephones to play music or games, surf the Internet, and even take photographs.

keep their people safe. Information about the economy, weather conditions, and public health is quickly shared. Telephones also allow international companies to conduct business without expensive travel.

Telephone communication makes the world seem smaller. Of course, this can have drawbacks. Quick, easy sharing means information can get into the wrong hands.

For this reason, keep your name, address, and other personal information safe. Never give it out to a stranger. With careful use, you can keep in touch and stay informed. This is all thanks to the telephone!

GLOSSARY

coordinate - to bring into a common action or movement.

current - the flow of electricity.

diaphragm (DEYE-uh-fram) - a thin, movable disk that vibrates either because of sound waves or to create them.

immigrate - to enter another country to live. A person who immigrates is called an immigrant.

microphone - a device that changes sound energy into electrical energy that can be transmitted or recorded.

Morse code - a code that uses dots and dashes, or long and short sounds, to represent letters of the alphabet, numbers, and punctuation marks. It is named for inventor Samuel F.B. Morse.

patent - the exclusive right granted to a person to make or sell an invention for a certain period of time.

portable - able to be carried or moved.

restriction - a limitation on something.

signal - a sound or an image transmitted in electronic communication, such as radio, telephone, or television. A signal is the wave or the current that transmits the message as well. Also, a signal may simply be an indication of something.

telecommunications - the science of sending messages over long distances by electronic means, as by telegraph, telephone, television, or computer.

telegraph - the equipment, process, and system used for communicating coded electric messages over wires.

unique - being the only one of its kind.

WEB SITES

To learn more about telephones, visit ABDO Publishing Company on the World Wide Web at **www.abdopublishing.com**. Web sites about telephones are featured on our Book Links page. These links are routinely monitored and updated to provide the most current information available.

INDEX

A
antenna 24, 25
anti-sidetone circuit 20

B
base unit 14, 25
batteries 14
Bell, Alexander Graham
    10, 11, 12
Bell Telephone Company
    12
Berliner, Emile 12

C
caller identification 22
careers 26
cellular telephones 13,
    14, 25
copper wiring 24
cord 14, 24
cordless telephones 14,
    24

D
dial tone 14
dialer 15, 22, 24
diaphragm 20, 22
display screen 22

E
Edison, Thomas A. 12
electrical signals 9, 16,
    17, 20, 21, 22, 24
electricity 8, 9, 10, 12, 14,
    17, 20, 21, 24

F
fiber-optic cables 24

H
handset 14

K
keypad 15, 22, 24

M
microphone 12, 16, 20
Morse code 8, 9

P
printed circuit board 17

R
radio waves 24, 25
receiver 17, 20, 22
ringer 16, 22
rotary dial telephones 15,
    22, 24

S
speaker 17, 22
switch hook 14

T
telegraph 8, 9
touch-tone telephones
    24
transmitter 12, 16, 17

W
Watson, Thomas A. 10,
    11
wires 9, 16, 20, 21